Zen O'clock

Zen O'clock

TIME TO BE

scott shaw

SAMUEL WEISER, INC.
York Beach, Maine

First published in 1999 by Samuel Weiser, Inc.
P. O. Box 612, York Beach, ME 03910-0612
www.weiserbooks.com

Library of Congress Cataloging-in-Publication Data
Shaw, Scott
Zen O'clock : Time to be / Scott Shaw.
p. cm.
Includes index.
ISBN 1-57863-124-6 (pbk. : alk. paper)
1. Zen meditations. I. Title.
BQ9289.S483 1999
294.3′4432--dc21 *98-54470*
CIP

Typeset in 11 point Berkeley
Printed in the United States of America
06 05 04 03 02 01 00
10 9 8 7 6 5 4 3 2
CA
The paper used in this publication meets all the minimum requirements of the American National Standard for Permanence of Paper for Printed Library Materials Z39.48–1984.

CONTENTS

Introduction	*vii*
Time	*1*
Life	*11*
Death	*53*
Emotions	*61*
Now	*83*
Desire	*103*
Perfection	*119*
Zazen	*125*
Index	*134*
About the author	*136*

INTRODUCTION

TIME—all of life is dominated by it.

TIME—every word, in all languages, is governed by it. But, what is it? The thinking mind has been programmed into believing that it is an object; that it does, in fact, exist.

TIME cannot be touched, it cannot be grasped or held onto. It can only be defined in terms of history; by what has happened in the past, even if that past was only a second ago. The majority of the world's people wish that this could be different.

TIME—in its purest form is simply a method to measure the distance between birth and death, for this interval known as life, is the only period where TIME may be consciously calculated.

When you exist, TIME exists. When you do not exist, TIME does not exist.

Modern society has placed a much greater value on TIME than this pure and simplistic description, however. We have chosen to create clocks, calendars, and schedules that we think we must exist within; making us excessively aware of the ever present passing of TIME.

TIME cannot be stopped. At best, it can only be witnessed.

Since it is human consensus that this concept of TIME exists, you must put it into perspective, learn to control it, as opposed to being controlled by it. To this end, take a few moments to read this book, take some more TIME to understand it. And, hopefully you, too, will come to a better comprehension of this process known as TIME and learn to live within it more peacefully.

CHAPTER ONE

Time

1

Where you are right now is where you are.

You may have a million developed desires to be in other places, doing other things, but you are not there, you are here.

Experience this moment to its fullest.

2

QUICK, CATCH IT!

This moment is gone; it can never be relived.

3

When you look forward into TIME,
it seems like forever.

When you look back into TIME,
it appears life has passed in a flash.

4

Can you see time?
No.

Then you should stop looking for it.

5

You can watch a clock tick.
You can witness a sunrise or a sunset.
But, that is not time. That is simply movement.

Movement is the defining factor of time.
From this on to that.
From that on to this.

6

Stop trying to observe time and
you will be free of time.

7

There is no beginning and there is no end to time.

There is only a beginning and an end
to your perception of time.

When you are alive you can witness time.
When you are dead you cannot.

Time is an ALIVE concept.

8

The judgment of time is always done
in the past tense.

You can only judge time in terms of placement—
comparing where you were then,
to where you are now.

9

The more you think and worry about time,
the more you will be controlled by it, and the faster it will appear to pass.
The less you concern yourself with time,
the freer you become,
and there is always plenty of time.

10

Can you save TIME?

No, there is no savings account for TIME.

11

There has always been a recorded history of TIME, whether it was recorded by human hands or written onto the surface of the earth.

Before that, did TIME exist?

Before your consciousness of TIME, did TIME exist?

12

Have you witnessed how sometimes TIME moves so slowly and other times it passes by so quickly?

TIME

During some periods of life one lives an enormous amount of experiences in a very short time. In these times of intensity, life goes by very fast.

At other times, life all seems to be the same; it passes quite slowly.

Make the best of each time period, for all life moves in cycles. Live and experience both fully while they are happening.

Live the fast time, as consciously as possible. Reflect upon all of these new experiences once TIME has slowed down.

13

If one could travel in TIME, either into the future or into the past, that would mean everything is continually happening forever.

Does this moment happen continually forever?

How can this moment be any place
other than where it is,
RIGHT HERE, RIGHT NOW?

14

Take the TIME to just do nothing.

It will open up a completely new world of insight for you.

CHAPTER TWO

Life

15

How many times have you stepped outside and not even noticed what the weather was like?

How many times have you traveled to some destination and, due to the fact that your mind was on another issue affecting your life, you did not even notice how you felt or what you saw?

How much of life do you let pass by without a thought?

16

Life is made up of experiences. Many of life's experiences are as momentary as the second in which they exist.

Feel them.
Live them.

17

Think of all of the times you took a shortcut in order to accomplish something.

What was the purpose?

It was probably so you could hurry up and get on to the next project or situation you believed needed your attention. Maybe you wished to be somewhere else, doing something else, and so you rushed. Whatever reasoning you may have possessed, by rushing through one subject and on to the next, you missed the beauty of living and experiencing the present moment fully.

18

"I can't wait!"

This is a common statement.

What's the hurry?

Do you get to where you are going any faster when you rush and make yourself upset?

No, you do not. You get there in the same amount of time as when you simply proceed to where you are going consciously.

■ ■ ■

If you relax, appreciate the beauty of where you are

now and plan your time wisely, arriving can become an enlightening experience, instead of creating a situation where you lose your peace by rushing.

19

Happiness is a choice.
Acceptance is a choice.
Forgiveness is a choice.
Anger is a choice.
Desire is a choice.
Love is a choice.
Life is a choice.

Your time, your choice.

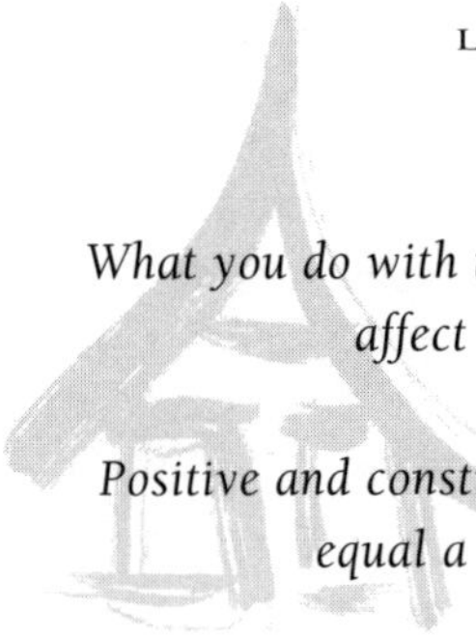

20

What you do with this moment does not only affect this moment.

Positive and constructive actions taken now equal a positive future.

Negative and destructive actions taken now create negative events in the future.

21

You are either getting better in this moment or you are getting worse.

Getting better is your choice.

It is what you choose to do with your time.

The simplest things lead you to getting better.

22

Some days pass by in their fullness,
others in their emptiness.

Empty or full is your perception of how you wish
your time to be spent.

A businessman desires a full day—
time spent interactive.

A monk desires an empty day—
time spent absorbed in solitude.

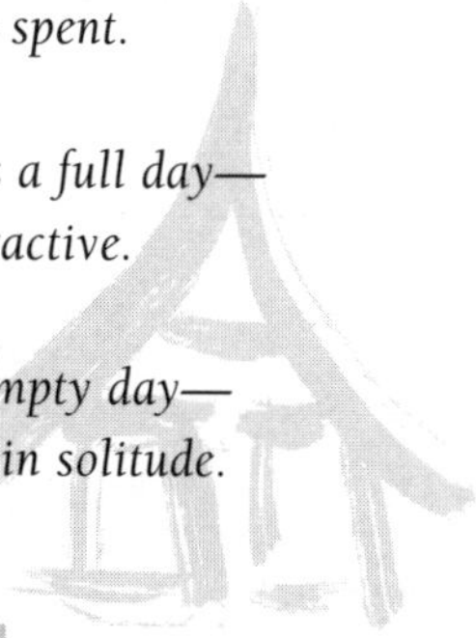

23

There are occasions when we allow ourselves a moment to just not care, times when we automatically sit back, view, and admire the beauty and perfection of the given moment. This feeling is different for each of us. It is a mental experience, but physical environments can help to bring it about.

Make a mental note when and where you encounter these experiences: perhaps being by the ocean, in the mountains, by a river; maybe just in some specific place alone. Wherever it is, give yourself some TIME, as often as you can make possible, to live those experiences.

The TIME will be well spent.

24

You can hold on to what you know, but there are no guarantees that what you know will exist in the next moment.

As long as you hold on to old beliefs, you keep yourself locked into one life position and you do not allow yourself the ability to have new experiences.

Why? Because you are expecting what you have known today to exist tomorrow.

Expectations of what will come tomorrow are hopeful speculation at best.
Tomorrow is promised to no one.
Life holds no guarantees.
Nothing lasts forever.

It can all change in a moment.

No matter how much you hold on to anything, there is nothing you can do to change the pattern of this world; sooner or later it will all be gone.

25

Pursuing something is good.
Choosing to pursue nothing is also good.
Being completely content with where you are, with what you have, is good.

Fantasize, dream all you want, but realize that you will never accomplish any of those desires if you do not map out a very conscious plan for their obtainment.

You can only fantasize about what you have been programmed into believing is desirable.

Dreams are nice, but if you do not attempt to live them, they will never be achieved and they will only cause you frustration.

If you have a desire, put your dream into action.

Is your TIME spent desiring, or is your TIME spent taking steps toward those desires?

26

Never allow yourself to think about what you could have done, had situations been different.

Situations were not different.
Don't waste your TIME.

You are HERE.
This is NOW.

You did not do "THAT" then, and nothing you can do will ever change it.

27

You cannot go back.
What's gone is gone. It can never return.
Lamenting will never bring about anything but unhappiness.

■ ■ ■

The past is gone.

It can never be changed and can only be relived in memories.

■ ■ ■

LIVE the moment NOW. Experience the moments to come, and let nothing further ever hold you back from encountering what you truly wish to experience.

28

It is your TIME; do with it what you will.

■ ■ ■

You find yourself in a traffic jam as you drive your car.
You find yourself waiting in an office for an appointment which should have occurred half an hour ago.
You are waiting for someone to arrive—who is very late.

What are you going to do—get angry?
Or, if you choose, you can put the time to the most beneficial use and accomplish something.

This accomplishment is only restricted by the limitations of your own anger keeping you from fully actualizing the moment.

If you are concerned about the lack of time, use every given situation to its fullest potential.

If you feel you must continually accomplish something, use every moment, do not let any moment slip by.

29

No one ever promised that life was fair.

The only time you feel cheated is when you expect something.

If you have no expectations you will possess no disappointments.

The less you expect, the freer you become, and the more you are not dominated by time. Why? Because you embrace acceptance.

Acceptance sets you free.

30

If you are always thinking about TIME, you will never have enough TIME.

People who rush throughout life find a LIFETIME quickly spent.

31

If you wonder how your TIME is spent—isolate it.

Set an alarm to go off every ten minutes.

Segregate your TIME and you will know where it goes.

32

If you have a problem with time, organize your time.

Take three notebooks:

NOTEBOOK ONE: *Write down what you hope to achieve in the given week.*

NOTEBOOK TWO: *Write down an hour-by-hour breakdown of what you desire to achieve each day.*

Be TIME realistic and be open to changes.
If you do not finish something on the specific desired day, move it forward to the next day
and be sure to make it a priority.
Then do it.

NOTEBOOK THREE: *As you go through the day, place in this notebook a complete schedule of what you did and what you accomplished at specific times. Add to it, briefly, how you felt about accomplishing the specified task.*

■ ■ ■

If you desire accomplishment, time yourself.
If you obtain what you desire,
does it make you happy?

If scheduling makes you anxious, leave the scheduling and the desire behind.

33

If you live by a schedule, if you make appointments, you must constantly think of time.

■ ■ ■

The majority of people live "morning logic." They are awakened by an alarm clock each day at the same time. They shower, shave, brush their teeth, put on their make-up, get dressed every day the exact same way. Then, they go to work. Afterward, they go home and watch television, go to a health club, or go out with friends. They then go to bed and await the alarm clock to start the same routine the next day. In this lifestyle there is never a new moment. This schedule is continued until death; though most people promise themselves someday it will be different .

■ ■ ■

Take a moment, envision your life without those programmed constraints. See yourself not needing to be structured or disciplined. Let your mind be at peace; forget where you are supposed to be, what you are expected to be doing. Ignore the fact, at least for this moment, that you have any place to ever be.

■ ■ ■

Allow yourself a moment of freedom and you, too, can find your own method for a livelihood not bound by time.

34

Relearn everything. Let every movement be new.

There are ways to survive without
the need for scheduling.

35

If you choose to stop living your life by the definition of scheduled time, you will enter into a space of freedom; worry and anxiety will leave you.

■ ■ ■

What is anxiety?
Concern about what is to come.

But, it has not happened yet and there is no proof that it ever will.

■ ■ ■

Set yourself free and no longer be concerned about anything which is not actually in progress— at this very moment.

36

Talk is cheap. What does it actually equal?

How much of your time do you spend discussing things that have no absolute meaning, or occurrences which you have no control over?

Creative discussions are interesting. It's a time to listen, to learn, to view opinions other than your own. It allows you a moment where everything else in your life can be forgotten.

Some people, however, allow continued meaningless conversations to dominate their life. This gives them a reason to procrastinate about their own unfulfilled desires.

Tape your own conversations; see what you say.

How do your words affect your LIFETIME?

37

Have you ever rushed to prepare for someone's arrival, feeling that he or she would soon be there and you would not be ready? You completed your preparation and your guest is not there on time or arrived very late.

In one period, you have rushed and time passed quickly. In the next, you were forced to wait and time progressed slowly.

Did the movement of time actually change? No, simply your perception of it changed.

38

Life holds many promises.

As long as you take no action and only hold on to daydreams, you will never experience what it is you may truly wish to live.

39

Take a look at others who have done what you think it is you wish to accomplish.

What is their lifestyle like?
What are they like?
Are they truly happy?

To be a business owner, is that what you desire?

To be dominated by external financial
influences and trends,
day in and day out until you die?

Lifetime secured employment at the same firm?
Twenty or thirty years of experiencing nothing
new or different?

To be famous?
Without the ability to do anything unnoticed.
Is that what you choose?

Reflect upon your life objectives deeply and analyze
them well before you place them into your
bank of desires.

40

If you view the mind of the average person, you will realize that most people choose to compete with one another, whether it be:

financially,
intellectually,
or in terms of physical beauty.

Most people do not even choose to realize that all things of this world are as temporary as life itself.

▪ ▪ ▪

If you remove competitive desires from your life and just live within your own peace and perfection, your TIME becomes your own and simple things will please you.

41

If you could do anything RIGHT NOW, at this moment, what would it be?

What is stopping you from doing it? With the exception of the unnecessary, unwanted, or unconscious involvement of others in your desire, you should go and do it.

42

Modern people generally fill their TIME with an occupation, mundane family involvements, car repairs, home maintenance, and the like. When they have any free time, they are generally so tired, they only wish to sleep.

Is that what life is truly about?

Most people are so self-involved with momentary necessities, they never take the TIME to truly witness what is going on in the world around them. The majority of people live in this grind throughout their existence. They choose to.
They tell themselves,

"This is the way life is."
"I am doing what I am expected to be doing."

That is a lie. It is your choice to do what you want with your TIME.

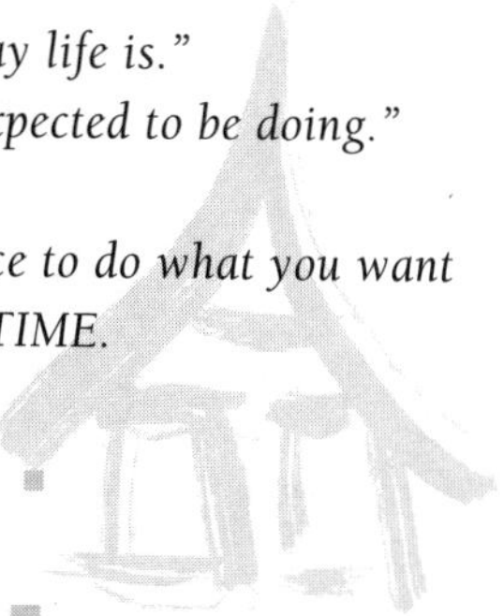

No one forces you to believe the lies of social acceptance in this world. The reason there is so little creativity and acknowledged genius is because the majority of people choose to believe the falsehood that they must forge out a living in the mainstream and, therefore, they have no TIME to live and create their dreams.

43

What if accomplishments meant nothing—if everything you did meant zero?

What would you choose to do?

In a sense this is the case of life.

Personal accomplishments are an illusion.

You will live, you will die, and that is that. When you are gone you can never reap the benefits or the gains of the particular human form you are currently in.

Even if you believe in reincarnation,
you will not be in the same body.

If you believe in Heaven and to get there you must be kind and good, that's fine; good is always good.

But, this world as you know it will cease to exist.

If all is here, then it is gone, what do you really want to do in the HERE?

Because the HERE is all that you can truly live.

44

Look at this moment—how many regrets do you have?
What are you going to do about them?

You have three choices:
One, you can sit around and feel miserable.
Two, you can do something to fix the damage
and achieve your preferred result.
Three, you can forget them.

■ ■ ■

It always seems that "later" you realize
what you should have done,
what you could have done.

What if you choose to view what you did,
simply as what you did,
what you had, as what you had,
what you lived, as what you lived,
and leave it at that?

45

Your desire may be for an experience lived in the past to be different from the actual event; but who knows what negative results you may have, in fact, incurred if you had lived the experience the way in which you desired it to be.

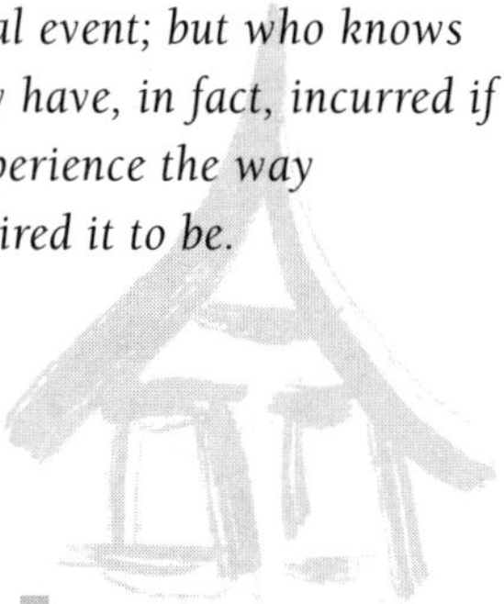

46

You are ALIVE.

It does not matter how old or how maimed you are,

as long as you are ALIVE, anything is possible.

■ ■ ■

People continually make excuses to themselves about why they cannot experience what they truly wish; for example:

"I'm not good enough,"
"I'm not intelligent enough,"
"I'm not holy enough," and so on.

You want something? Do it!
Forget all the excuses. Make a game plan
and go after it.

The pursuit of it will give you a feeling of
accomplishment and the experience of taking control
over your LIFETIME.

It is the greatest healer.

47

Tomorrow is always a new day.

Make it a new day, don't bring negative experiences
from the past into it.

48

One choice leads to the next set of available circumstances.

With a conscious mind, you can do anything.

49

Life is a step-by-step process.

You didn't know then what you know now because you were not prepared to know it then.

■ ■ ■

See your life as an overall passageway.

Don't look back with regrets, because there is nothing that you can do to change the past.

Do not look forward with anticipation.
Do it or don't do it.
Live it, when it arrives.

■ ■ ■

Live the perfection of this moment and the next moment will take care of itself.

You will grow. Life will continue. And, in the end there will be no regrets, for you will have lived what you have lived.

50

TIME is a scale we created in order to measure our worldly accomplishments.

TIME makes you rush to accomplish something.
TIME makes you believe you should be accomplishing something other than what you have already done.

■ ■ ■

Accomplishments, no matter what you call them, even that of being on a holy crusade, are only as temporary as your life.

Great artists, scientists—and even holy men—also die.

51

Ultimately, life cannot be fully understood.

■ ■ ■

As humans, we wish to find an explanation for every occurrence that transpires in the world around us. All of these conclusions, however, are simply rationalizations of the thinking mind. Therefore, they are influenced by the science and accepted knowledge of the present time.

■ ■ ■

Forget attempting to understand each life occurrence and you will be a thousand times freer.

Witness occurrences, but do not become lost in seeking their definition. Instead, live each moment of your life as consciously as possible—accepting its perfection—and choose to be happy with it. From this, you will not be controlled by the desire for anything to be any different than it actually is. The need for feeling regret or giving thanks will, thereby, vanish.

If you come to understand an occurrence, great.
If you do not come to understand an occurrence, great.

All is Perfect. Live the Perfection.

52

Through practice you can learn to alter
your perception of TIME;
intentionally slow it down or speed it up
when it is necessary.
How? Simply do it.

All of life is individual perception.
Each experience is what you make of it.

Isolate the moments of your life when
TIME passes quickly.
Isolate the moments of your life when
TIME passes slowly.

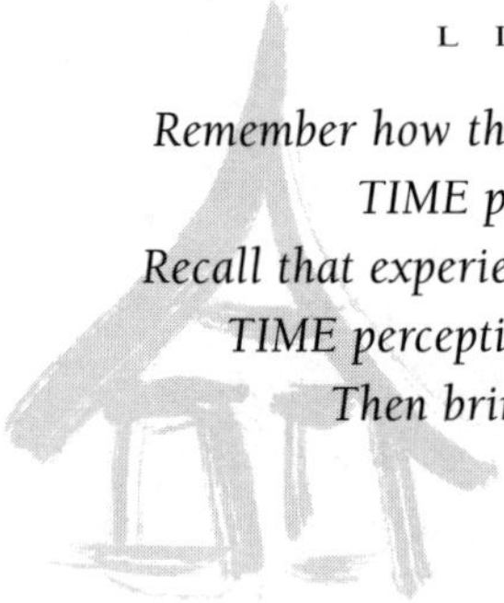

Remember how the experience of each
TIME period felt.
Recall that experience, when one of the
TIME perceptions is necessary.
Then bring it about.

CHAPTER THREE

Death

53

Life is lived.

Death is not lived, though its coming may be experienced.

54

There is birth, there is the limited time in between, and then there is death. It's as simple as that.

No matter how much you may want it to be another way, this will not change.

55

We all, if we live long enough, will become old.

Life is a continuum, a process.

Age is a perspective, a point of view which you have decided upon.

■ ■ ■

When you are young, you desire to be older.
When you are old, you desire to be younger.

How quickly the old forget their youthful desire for age.

■ ■ ■

The young believe that there is always a tomorrow.
The old witness that tomorrow may never come.

The young, hesitate.
The old, rush.

The young have no need to hurry, as they believe they will have the time and ability to accomplish everything they desire.

The old witness the impending curtain of death and, thus, must hurry to accomplish all that remains to be done.

56

What is it that makes you think you will live on forever in Heaven or through reincarnation? Was this philosophy an original thought? Did you possess either of these concepts when you were an infant? No, you were not born with this mindset. These promises came later, when religious doctrines and philosophic ideas were introduced to you.

These concepts were recorded many generations ago. But, what makes them valid and why do different schools of religious philosophy possess different ultimate outcomes? Is one right and the other wrong? And, who is to say?

The only thing that makes any system of thought valid is your own belief in the system.

What is it that makes you want to live forever?

Because life is all that you have ever known.

57

Is the person who desires death, due to a distaste for life, free from desire? No. He is full of desire for his LIFETIME *to be different.*

Change your life experience as opposed to choosing to end LIFE'S TIME.

Do not let the ways of the material world win.

58

We all will die.
Birth equals death.
The time in between is all
that we have.

■ ■ ■

Physical death will come. It comes to us all. We all need to come to terms with that fact. There is nothing anyone can do to stop it. Our only defense is to live this moment as consciously as possible and do what we truly wish to do. Then, when the time to die arrives, we leave this body with a free heart and a liberated mind.

59

If you knew when you were going to die, how would you NOW be living your TIME?

CHAPTER FOUR

Emotions

60

Anger is an emotion.
Emotions last only for a limited period of time.

Why let something so temporary take control of you and make you say and do things which may remain with you long past the moment this emotion is experienced?

61

All emotions are momentary, they will come and then they will go.

Do not believe that you are bound to them forever.

In time, any emotional experience, no matter how profound, will pass and you will wonder how you could have ever been controlled by it.

62

Happiness is an emotion.

It is you who chooses to be happy or unhappy in any given moment.

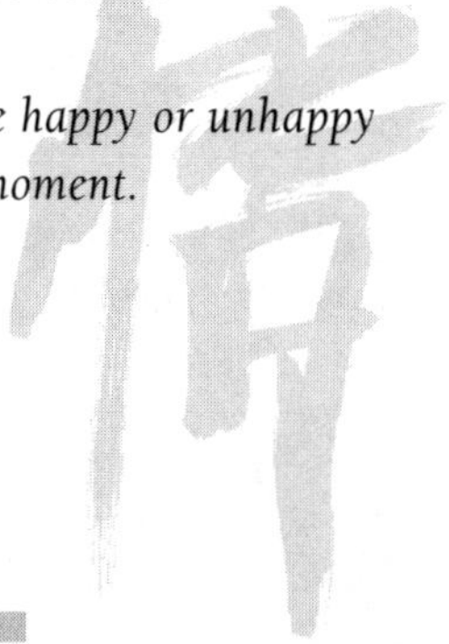

63

Have you ever observed somebody having
a really good time?
Have you ever watched two people in love?

Their TIME is filled with fullness.

■ ■ ■

Enjoyment and love are both emotions. They are decided upon reactions to a given set of circumstances.

Are you forced to enjoy any specific event?
Does any person possess the ability to force you
to love them?

In each case the answer is, "No."
You choose to enjoy.
You choose to love.

Reach inside and feel the place in you that experiences enjoyment. Go to that place in you where love dwells. Take these emotions out. Allow yourself to experience them, RIGHT NOW.

You will come to understand that you can be inside of any situation and convince yourself to enjoy it. See any person and feel total love.

Emotions belong to you. You can turn them on and off at will.

64

Allow No-One and No-Thing the power to control your TIME.

When you possess reoccurring negative emotions toward any individual or event, you allow that negative experience to be continually relived in your life. It, therefore, becomes a dominant focal point of your mindset. Thus, you are allowing the negative person or event to maintain an unnecessary presence in your LIFETIME.

Do they deserve to be allowed this dominating presence?

65

It is your own choice to allow any person or situation to have lasting negative emotional control over you. You can stop reliving any experience if you just say, "STOP IT," to yourself each time the thought comes to your mind. Then, immediately begin to consciously think about something very positive that has happened in your life.

■ ■ ■

Forgive and you will be free.
Forget and you will be freer.

66

Some people choose to blame others for their own physical and emotional state of being.

Thus, they allow someone outside themselves to take control over the moments of their life.

■ ■ ■

If you choose to believe that other people are at fault for your current state of existence, this means that you are allowing another individual to maintain unwanted control over you. STOP IT!

No one can have any control over you unless you allow it—not your parents, not your employer, not your spouse, not your lover, not a criminal, not the bad driver in front of you.

Foolish and power-hungry individuals may, in fact, attempt to control a specific moment of your time, either by unconscious actions or a predetermined motivation, but it is you who can block them from having long term control over your life. How do you achieve this? Simply leave negative situations and never look back.

The best defense to consciously retaliate against people you believe have wronged you—

Become better than they are.

67

Emotions are addictive. They can be allowed to dominate your TIME.

68

Emotions do not equal life.
Emotions equal emotions.
Emotions are dominated by external life situations.
Emotions create external life situations.
Emotions are temporary, no matter how much you allow a specific emotion to dominate your lifetime.

Allow your choices about your own emotions to set you free.

69

Situations that you do not like may occur in your life.
That is a common consensus with everyone.

You may have a preference for a past situation to have been lived out differently than it actually was. That, too, is very common.

You have the power to choose—to discriminate—as to whether or not you will allow these momentary situations to affect you longer than just their passing moments in TIME.

■ ■ ■

Witness unwanted moments and let them pass.

70

Whenever you remember something that angered you in the past, you can decide to see it for what it is—a learning experience, an experience that led you on the path to becoming a more complete individual.

You will be free from the pain if you allow yourself to be free from the pain.

71

You may not feel happy in this moment,
but moments pass.

■ ■ ■

Why don't you feel happy right now?

What would change this negative feeling for you?

What if you decided to just change your mind about your feelings RIGHT NOW? You could choose to live this moment with the emotion of love—appreciating it for whatever it's worth!

■ ■ ■

Life is your choice, your "decided-upon" mental attitude.
Take control of your emotions. Do not allow something so temporary as a negative emotion to dominate you, even for a second of your LIFETIME.

72

It is you who decides how to react a certain way to any life situation.

You can choose to feel anything you want:
peace when you are angry,
happiness when you are sad,
love for a person whom you previously hated.

This is your TIME; consciously choose
to make the best of it.

73

Instead of experiencing guilt, or making excuses for your previous negative actions, start RIGHT NOW to perform positive actions.

74

Negative emotions serve as a hindrance for moving toward the completion of any project, be it physical or spiritual.

Some people continually put psychological obstacles in their own path of completion.

If a project is not completed in a generally realistic period of time, you can then feel a negative self-gratifying emotion in saying, "I knew I couldn't do it."

Allowed to continue, this pattern becomes a defining factor in your life.

"Accomplishment Perfection" is understanding that a task is completed when it is completed.

All things are completed when they are completed.

Do them. But, don't worry about doing them.

75

What others think and perceive of you—
The fashion statement you are attempting to make—
What is the current trend?
What is momentarily acceptable?
Are you liked?
Are you disliked?
Loved?

Unloved?
Are you beautiful or ugly?

All of these things are time-robbing excuses and obstacles based in your own induced psychological inadequacies.

Ultimately, who but you really cares?

76

Human beings do many things to be accepted. People devote entire lives to momentary physical pursuits. They may not even take the time to realize what they are doing.

Take, for example, the woman who is a devoted wife for many years and then her mate leaves or dies—her life is destroyed, for the devotion toward her partner was all she ever pursued.

Or, the boy who is enticed into a life of crime, attempting to be accepted by his peers. From this, he ends up injuring others and spending many years in a correctional facility.

Or, perhaps, the employee, who works his or her entire life for a company, only to have it go out of business, or force the employee into an early retirement.

Then there are people who are lost in appearing attractive to others—they make their hair just right, or wear lots of make-up every day, hoping that someone will notice them.

Who do you live your LIFETIME for?

77

People live, then they die.
Situations change.
What is commonly accepted is different
in every culture;
different, in every defined period of time.
Trends and styles come and go.

What is one left with? In all cases, only yourself.

You are not that illusionary physical and emotional
shell that you are wearing.

78

Many people choose to be superficial. They search for beauty in the eyes and arms of others. They desire to find acceptance from the congratulations of the outside world. They spend the TIME of their lives in this pursuit.

This superficial pursuit is a source of shame and embarrassment.

Shame and embarrassment are created by your desire to be seen in a different way than you actually are at any given moment.

You are what you are.
You are who you are.

This is the reality that you are living—
as momentary as it may be.

Accepting this—does it really matter how others judge you in a given moment of TIME?
Does someone else's appraisal of you mean more to you than your own understanding of yourself?

How free would you be if you just didn't care what others thought or felt about you?

79

Do you attempt to live up to other's expectations?

Or do you live your own TIME?

80

How do you view other people?

Do you judge them in the same way as you feel you have been judged?

■ ■ ■

Take a moment to understand how you view others.
Do you judge them by:
Beauty? Clothing?
Wealth? Intelligence?
Position?

■ ■ ■

Judgment takes TIME.
How free would you become if you simply allowed others to be whoever it is that they are?

CHAPTER FIVE

Now

81

No matter how much you are in the Here and Now, by the time you realize it, that Now is gone.

The majority of experiences in this life pass by in a blur.

There are a million things going on at the same time and it is impossible to witness them all.

Experience each moment as completely as possible.

To experience each moment as completely as possible is a developed habit. You must practice it.

82

When you are caught up in the blur of a rapidly paced life, the Here and Now still exists.

Your Here and Now is simply dominated by the complexity of the life you have created for yourself.

83

It becomes an obsession of the mind to attempt to find time to accomplish all the tasks you deem it necessary to complete.

What if you simply believed there was nothing to accomplish?

Would you not then be free and your mind not obsessed with the necessity to complete your goals?

Try lying down and just not caring.

Spend a day just allowing yourself to do whatever your body and mind suggest.

84

If your clock is broken, what TIME *is it?*

85

Freeze TIME *and what do you have?*

Nothing.

86

Workers time themselves.
Students time themselves.
Lovers time themselves.
Meditators time themselves.

If you have nowhere to be and nothing to prove, there is no need to time yourself.

87

Time changes things—
people,
places.

Memories recapture events. But, memories are not the NOW.

You go to a place one time and the memories of the events which took place there are very clear and defined. You return to the same place a second and third time, and memories of the events that took place become blurred.

People oftentimes remember the same event differently. Why? Because their perception of the event was filtered through their own emotional understanding.

Over long periods of time, people confuse the events that actually took place with the way they wish the events would have unfolded.

Memories lie.

The NOW cannot lie.

88

Virtually all spiritual teachings claim that meditation is very beneficial.

Instead of closing your eyes and retreating, try opening your eyes and truly witnessing all that is in front of you.

Take a moment right where you are, RIGHT NOW:

What do you see?

What do you smell?
What do you feel?

Look everywhere. See and experience everything.

Look at things you have seen a million times as if you have never seen them before.

89

Meditate in the NOW.

Witness the outside, but know the inside.

Sense each part of your body—your hands, your legs, your chest, your head.

What do they feel like?
What are they experiencing?

Look deeply into your mind.

What's in there?
Who are you?
What are your emotions and why?

The majority of people never learn how to truly feel or experience anything but momentary emotional stimuli.

Meditate on the NOW anytime the thought comes to your mind and you will learn to experience the NOW.

■ ■ ■

TIME will be witnessed as your vehicle to feeling.

90

Whether you love or hate what you are doing—
feel it,
live it,
know it inside and out.

Witness every aspect of the actions you take—and all the effects created by your action.

91

If you discontinue living your life in terms of tomorrows, then all things will be lived NOW.

"I will do it then."
"I cannot accomplish it now."

The "I wills," and the "I cannots."

These ideas are conditions which many people have allowed themselves to believe.

Do what you are going to do NOW!

The motivation for any accomplishment is there if you choose for it to be there.

92

Preparing for . . .

Waiting for . . .

There is no guarantee that those times will ever come.

When you are dreaming of what is to come tomorrow—and not moving toward your desires now—you are assuming that tomorrow will be there, and that you will have the time and the capacity to accomplish your desires, then.

By living your life in this fashion you will never possess your dreams and you will never have the ability to truly experience a full and fulfilled life. Thus, you will forever be bound by the vice of time.

Someday there will be no more tomorrows for you.

Live your life NOW!

93

Why are you doing anything other than what you want to do RIGHT NOW?

Do not make excuses to yourself—

responsibility,
making someone else happy,
doing something for the money,
because you were taught this is the way it's supposed to be.

Do what you want to do.

No excuses.

Doing what you want to do leads to freedom.
Freedom leads to enlightenment.

94

There is no such thing as wasted TIME.

You are living what you are living RIGHT NOW.

You cannot be any place other than where you are, though you may desire it to be so.

■ ■ ■

If you could be elsewhere, where would it be?
What would be there that is not here?
What will being there prove?

Ultimately, you do not know, because you are not there. You are only expecting a situation or person to be present, elsewhere.

There is no guarantee, however, that any desired result will ever take place.

Nothing is ever the way you expect it to be.

95

This moment is equally as important as all others in your lifetime.

Live it and experience it fully.

96

There are times in life when we are instantly sent into the experience of NOW.

These times are generally brought about at moments of pure intensity, be they good or bad.

In the forced NOW—TIME appears to progress very slowly and every second, every one of your thoughts is acutely witnessed.

■ ■ ■

NOW, is a mental place. It occurs either spontaneously or by a very conscious choice.

NOW can only happen when you are not thinking of other things, when your mind is not desiring to be in any other place.

97

As one grows older, each movement of life becomes expected, as each sight has been previously witnessed. Thus, to many, life has become boring and all of life's actions are predictable.

■ ■ ■

Look around yourself, see everything as if you are seeing it for the first time. Let yourself know the amazement. Allow yourself to feel love for everything in your field of vision.

Watch the perfection as it is happening.

98

Forget what you have learned.
Forget what you know.

Live all of life as a new experience and
you will be free.

Free from worry.
Free from expectation.
Free from previously gained understandings.
Free from earlier experiences that hold you bound to
the positive or negative aspects of other
people or external events.

Let everything in life be new.

■ ■ ■

It is unfair to new acquaintances and to new occurrences to introduce them to the gains and the pains of previously known experiences. By doing this, you rob the freedom and spontaneity from any new life moment.

■ ■ ■

Wake up and feel a new day.
Live and feel a new life.
Look into new eyes and experience all the possibilities.

CHAPTER SIX

Desire

99

Siddhartha Gautama, the Sakyamuni Buddha,
profoundly stated,
"The cause of suffering is desire."

Goals are desire;
Possessions are desire;
Conquests are desire;
Love is a desire;
Relationships are desire;
Accomplishments are desire;
Enlightenment is a desire.

100

Your life is your choice. You can put yourself in an arena of desire, wasting all your time wishing to be

more powerful, richer, younger, older, more accomplished, whatever, or you can simply let life take its course,
do what needs doing, and be free.

How do you free yourself from desire?

DON'T CARE.

It is you who chooses to care or not to care.

101

Imagine no desire for accomplishment.

Imagine no desire to be anything or in any place which you are not currently in.

Imagine having everything you want
RIGHT HERE,
RIGHT NOW,
this very moment.

This does not mean to visualize or fantasize that you have more than you currently possess, for that negates the beauty of this moment.

Simply decide to not desire more than what is currently in your possession:
financially,
physically,
or spiritually.

It is very easy to achieve. It is a state of mind.

Simply believe that it is so and it is so.

102

Desire for anything to be different is what holds one bound to time.

103

Desires are NOW.

If you did not have that desire, think how free you would be.

Stop where you are, RIGHT NOW.
First, think about any desires you currently possess:

new possessions;
new relationships;
new positions.

Bring all of them clearly into focus in your mind.
Now, instantly, forget them completely.
Let go of all desires you may be holding.

Look around yourself—feel this moment.
Feel how free you have become without that desire?

104

When you relieve yourself of all desire,
this moment becomes perfect.

105

You choose your own desires.
No one puts them in your mind.

Even if others have influenced you, which is the case with all of us, it is you who chooses to think what you think and desire what you desire.

If it is not you putting those thoughts in your mind, those desires in your heart, then who is it?

106

Make the process of getting where you choose to be as meaningful and important to your own heart as obtaining your desired goal.

■ ■ ■

If you believe your life will be vastly different when you obtain whatever goal it is that you seek, you are wrong. Life is a step-by-step process, one step leading to the next. It does not change, all of a sudden, when a specific goal is obtained, though many have falsely led you to believe that this is the case.

Many people have enormous fantasies built up about what their lives will be like when they reach their desired plateau. If and when they ever get there, it is never what they have imagined.

If you can allow yourself to love and experience every moment of life, no matter where you are in your own scale of desired perfection, and not wish that it be any different, then you will be free, and the time scale of goal-setting will not hold you unnecessarily bound. You will have already achieved the ultimate objective—for your present moment will be a place of peace, happiness, and fulfillment.

107

If you decide to want nothing more than what you have RIGHT NOW, you are free. You can pass from moment to moment without unnecessary worry.

You do whatever it is you do—that is fine; it is the nature of life. But, your actions do not hold you bound unnecessarily to the cause and effect of this material world. Tomorrow you may be gone, but with a heart free of desire, that is all right with you, as well.

By living with this mindset, the promises of fame, fortune, eternal youth, and forever in reincarnation or Heaven, have no meaning to you.

108

Desires are dominated by TIME.

You can only experience them when you have the TIME to dream.

You can only daydream when your mind is unleashed and you are not involved in accomplishing something.

109

What is prayer?
Asking for desires that you believe to be worthy.

What is time?
What you live, while seeking your desires.

110

You want what you want, NOW!
We all want what we want, NOW!
That is human nature.

In some cases you may have the ability to achieve your desire in this given moment.
In other cases, you will not.

What is this desire that makes you hold onto your dream and wish for something other than the perfection you have the ability to feel
RIGHT NOW?

Why must you have it?
Will it be as important tomorrow?
Will it still matter if you are alive five years from today?

111

How many times have you been doing one thing and wishing you were doing another?

How many times have you been doing another thing and wishing you were doing what you once wished you were not doing?

Life is like this puzzle. Desires pull us in a million directions at one time.

What we want this moment is not what we will want in the next moment.

The only desire that lasts forever is one that has not yet been fulfilled; because that is the one which is not known, felt, or experienced. Thus, it has not had the chance to become boring, commonplace, and mundane.

Whatever exists in this moment, love it,
and you will be free.

112

To say you desire something is fine. Everyone, no matter how holy they claim to be, desires something.

Even desiring nothing is desiring something.

Are you going to let that desire control you?
What will it mean if you achieve it?
What may the later unforeseen cost of it be?

113

Everything falls into its own framework and ultimate perfection.

Nothing is whole within itself.

One step leads to the taking of the next.

This moment leads to the one after.

A desire will give birth to the need for another desire.

Your desire, your choice.

114

Life's time is spent in the fulfillment of your needs and your desires; whether they are absolute necessities like food, drink, and sleep, or personal desires like possessions, entertainment, enlightenment, fame, and fortune.

There is no way to win this battle.
DON'T FIGHT IT.

Being in a body holds you absolutely bound to NEEDS.

Accept them, but don't be dominated by them.

CHAPTER SEVEN

Perfection

115

Life is perfect.
Can you see the perfection?

Good or bad is all a point of view and a state of mind.

You make the decision what to like or dislike.

If you love Hell, it becomes Heaven.

116

Certainly, we all can see this moment does not last an eternity.

If we examine life closely, we can find some good in what is commonly considered bad, and some bad in all that is seen as good. It is simply a perception.

What is not seen as perfection in this moment may well be understood as having been the perfect event to occur in your lifetime at a later point in time.

One action leads to the next.

117

Have you ever noticed how sometimes, though you may have disliked an initial experience, it led you to something positive—something else, someone else, something more.

Without that initial negative experience, you never would have moved forward and on to something positive.

118

Don't hold on to a momentary satisfaction or the lack of temporary sensory gratification.

If you take a moment to step back and see beyond your own momentary desires, then the perfection of life is witnessed.

119

Things are accomplished in their own TIME.

Where progress is—RIGHT NOW—is perfect.

When you accept this, you will be free from Completion Anxiety and the unnecessary disquieting of your mind.

120

All life is perfect and as it should be.

Each life experience falls into its own placement and leads you to your next step forward in TIME.

Accept this understanding and you are free.

CHAPTER EIGHT

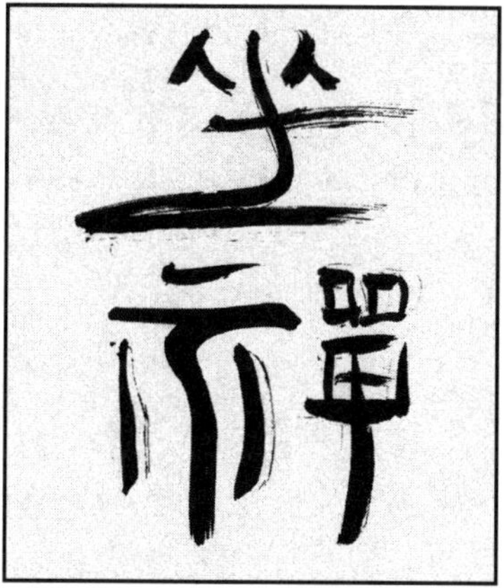

Zazen

121

Zazen means to sit in Zen.

Zen is the functional suchness of this individually perceived abstract reality that we call life.

■ ■ ■

Zazen is the word used to define seated meditation.

Meditation teaches you to turn off your thinking mind.

While you meditate, you think of nothing; thus, you desire nothing.

In that time you are free.

122

Through the teaching of Zen we come
to understand that
emotions are temporary,
desires are temporary,
and even life is temporary.

Zazen teaches us to forego the emptiness upon which human existence is based, so we can embrace the cosmic wholeness of the universe.

123

Zazen is not a complicated process.

Sit down in a comfortable position.
Close your eyes.

Experience how the closing of your eyes separates you from the physical world around you.

Feel the serenity of not being dominated by what you see.

124

With your eyes closed, witness your thinking mind.

Who is thinking?
Is it the physical person which you identify
as your body?
Is it the individual who desires all the material objects
and life attainments?
Or is it a spiritual essence that lies deeply removed
from the constraints of the physical world?

Embrace your inner being.

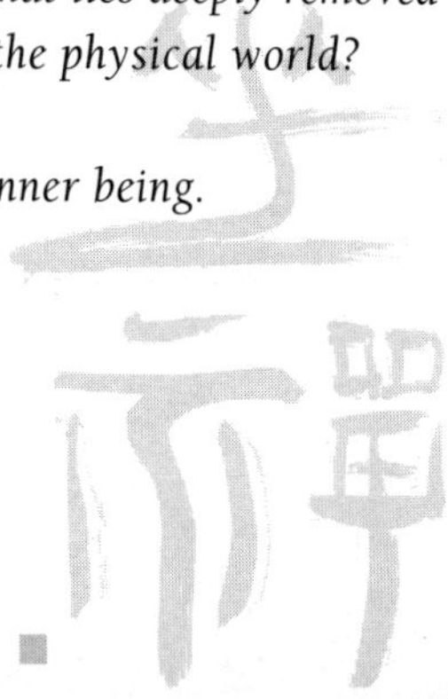

125

As you meditate, watch your thoughts flow like the waves of the ocean crashing upon the sea shore. They come in, and then just as naturally, they go out.

Realize that they are not you.
You are not your thoughts.

126

Witness your thoughts flowing away into the great abyss of suchness.

Embrace the freedom of mental emptiness.

127

*Begin to witness life-giving breath enter and
exit your body.
With each in breath, count the number One.
With each out breath, count the number Two.*

128

*In Zazen, forget to think,
as thinking is only thinking—it holds you back from
embracing the divine.*

■ ■ ■

*If a thought comes to your mind, witness it disappear
like an eagle flying away
in the vast blue sky.*

Refocus and again count "One," "Two."

129

From Zazen comes one thought.

The thought of no thought.

No thought exists when you do not care
if there is a past or a future.

As no time exists, Satori is born.

130

Satori is embraced when time is absent.

How do you move beyond time? Zazen.

Embrace the perfection of conscious nothingness.

CONCLUSION

This is your TIME.
Live it.

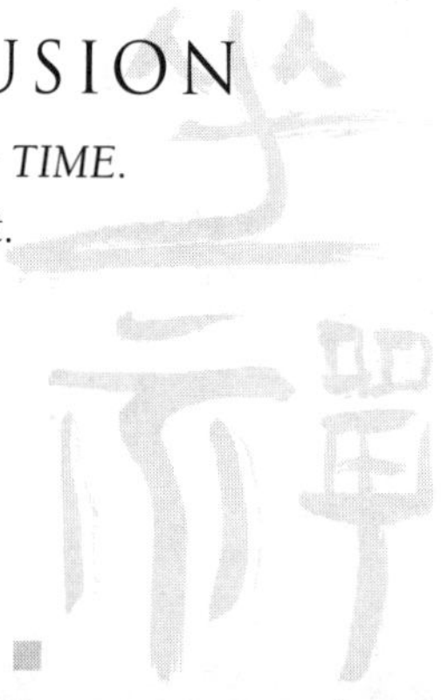

INDEX

accomplishment, 28, 40, 48, 105
- *perfection, 76*

actions, 16
- *negative, 74*

age is a perspective, 55
anger, 24, 62
anxiety, 31
beauty, 18
- *appreciate, 14*

beginning, 4
business owner, 35
choice, 15, 46, 65, 104
clock, 4
completion anxiety, 122
conscious nothingness, 133
consciousness, 12
control, 68
conversations, meaningless, 33
creative discussions, 33
daydreams, 35, 112
death, 54, 59
desires, 21, 28, 36, 58, 80, 94, 104, 108, 112-116, 127
do nothing, 10
dreams, 20, 21, 94
emotions, 62, 64, 69, 127
- *negative, 66, 73, 75*

emotional stimuli, 91
employment, secured, 36
enlightening experience, 15
enlightenment, 95
excuses, 95
expectations, 26
experiences, 12, 18, 23, 84
experiencing the present moment fully, 13
forgiveness, 67
freedom, 30, 31, 90, 100, 110
getting better, 16
good, 20
guarantees, 19
guilt, 74
happiness, 63, 74
here and now, 84
I can't wait, 14
ideas, philosophic, 57
intensity, 8
interactive, 17

INDEX

judging others, 82
life
envision your, 30
is fair, 25
moves in cycles, 6
is temporary, 127
live now, 23
love, 64, 74
meditation, 89, 90, 91, 126, 130
memories, 23, 87, 89
momentary necessities, 39
morning logic, 29
movement, 4
new day, 45
notebooks, 27
obstacles, psychological, 75
pain, 72
peace, 74
perception, 17, 34, 50, 121
of time, 5
perfection, 99, 110, 116, 120
of this moment, 47
prayer, 112
promises, 35
pursuit, superficial, 80
rationalizations, 49
reincarnation, 41, 57
religious doctrines, 57
responsibility, 95
right here, right now, 9
scheduling, 28, 31
situations, negative, 69
solitude, 17
sunrise, 4
talk is cheap, 32
thinking, 131
time
does it exist, 7
filling, 38
tomorrow, 56
traffic, 24
waiting, 24
weather, 12
witness, 90, 92, 130
worry, 31
you are here, 2
Zazen, 126, 128
sitting, 128

Scott Shaw is a true modern day mystic. From a young age, he has devoted his life to the experience of realization. Born in Los Angeles, he continually travels to Asia, documenting obscure aspects of Asian culture, in words and on film, and refining his knowledge of meditative understanding. He believes that one must make the mundane an exercise in mysticism and everyday living the ultimate teacher of cosmic consciousness.